Turnstile Burlesque

John Greiner

Turnstile Burlesque

Poems ©2017 by John Greiner
facebook.com/john.greiner.31
all rights reserved by the author

Cover art by Steven B. Smith
agentofchaos.com & walkingthinice.com

Crisis Chronicles #91
ISBN: 978-1-940996-43-1
1st edition, 1st printing, 100 copies

Published 2 June 2017 by
Crisis Chronicles Press
3431 George Avenue
Parma, Ohio 44134 USA

crisischronicles.com
ccpress.blogspot.com
facebook.com/crisischroniclespress

Special thanks to *Burp* and *Newtown Literary*, where a selection of the poems included in this book originally appeared.

Contents

Music
The History of Painting
Slip the Sky
Afternoon Transgression
An Hour from the Burning Bush
Colossuses Clutter the Seasons
Tuba
Promenade
Iberian Autumn
All-American
Jane in Her Business Suit
This Being an Odd Day
Market Day
Cessation Special
Onset and Onslaught
Luscious
Triangle
She Was a Study in Wind Patterns
Stoop Sale
Lunch Break
El
Leopard Skin Coat
Frankie, the Airplanes Are Diving
Still Dark
Coney Island Solstice Extension

Music

The Equestrian has fallen from his mount,
                  forgotten Savannah
      and cares not in the least for the sea.
Horse and hero are nowhere to be found.
That angel doesn't have the time
        for Bergdorf's,
                nor the cold cash.
Winter nerves hammer while standing
          next to the nearest war story
                  I've been told to fear.
Freezing and covered in fur,
        I'm an Inuit dreaming of
                      the stars
                              that only show
            during blackouts.
Park Avenue is burning
              with Christmas
                    want merciless pomp
                              well lit.
There's more than enough jesters about
            even if the Mayflower Shoppe
                  is long gone and forgot.
              It is so meaningless to eat
        and yet I grow fatter by the day.
She stares, too down to be celestial,
              takes in the portrait
                      by Cecilia Beaux,
a minor model caught
in a gilded age not her own.

The History of Painting

My shoe is loose,
       the left one.
I do not tighten
       the string.
My shoe,
my shoestring
and all of my fears
of tripping,
falling over,
hitting the floor
do not flee
my thoughts,
even though
my laces are double
knotted.
Western culture is on
       its way to obliteration.
Soon, all paintings
       will be dirty fingerprints
too sticky to touch.

Slip the Sky

Lower the Ceiling!
I slip the sky.
Radio leak
(you won't realize).
Staircase to New York City.
I'll summer without my hat,
traveling from borough
to borough, sneaking glances
in hallway mirrors to straighten
my hair and when I'm
through, Mary, Queen
of Siberian souls, boredom
and Brighton Beach will be ours.

Afternoon Transgression

I found
      myself
      lost
in the armor
of your eyes   with a memory
                                coughed up.
            You always said
            I was a gorgeous
                                    rodent
banished   from the granaries of paradise
because of my lust
      for the chimera
of a cheese sandwich.

An Hour from the Burning Bush

Where I stood was an hour
from the burning bush
that's what the compass
and the guide book said
the sun was setting
and I was short of matches
so I was shit out of luck
I should have never fallen in
with the Biblical scholars
who were always asking
me for the money for an egg
cream over on 2nd Avenue
the alchemists were better
behaved the kind of masters
that my mother would have
preferred to see me smoke
cigarettes with none of this
really mattered in the middle
of nowhere with Moses
far from sight and most likely
forgotten by everyone out
in the wilderness but myself

Colossuses Clutter the Seasons

Turning   startled   the
                city pink
                and up there the
                sky Union Square
what generals we once had
she said   swinging around   laughing
in a general way
there was an hour of fear   at the very beginning
                of the battle
              but the historians
            couldn't describe it
      with its graceful rushes
and exquisite falls
            so we were left with nothing but sizable
            myths and all the colossuses that
            clutter the seasons of depositions
what an hour it must have been
now there are street lamps
and a security
that makes for a good
              lunch spot
murderers and heroes
captains of the imagination
tall tales   Paul Revere and Pinkerton agents
          Buffalo Bill Cody and William Calley
          Green Mountain Boys and Steven Green
whiff of perfume
             passing
             towards the hum
                      in the distance
she said   someday there will be   a tumble
and talk of hours to come

Tuba

Having seized hold of the tuba,
                I hollowed out a melody
that the boys at Eastman (and Kodak)
                        asserted would serve
as the salacious score to the century
                unspecified.
This astounded the kids in the corner
        who were decent percussionists
                in spite
      of their youthful lack of splashy cymbals.
Everyone wanted to talk with their high hats
                            hit
of Dodo Marmorosa,
   Don Byas,
   Duck Dunn,
   Dvořák,
the Kinks,
   Khachaturian,
   Kurt Cobain
and finally Commander Cody
and His Lost Planet Airmen.
                  I had to blast my horn
                  because it was the high holidays
                  in the brass balls age
and being a man a la mode
I was antsy to scratch my sound
                onto the streets,
which is exactly what I did,
after closing the spit valve.

Promenade

    Seen
    fine new
    city New
    York
weather fresh as a schoolgirl
        out and about
        beauty
        punch
        line
today
        my
        timing's off
her swagger plays
        on
long lost
        autumn
        walks in
        the wild

Iberian Autumn

Spanish heart
    the peninsular Armada
artichokes in olive oil
  pour poor Portuguese girl
    blue eyed Iberian
the caravan has arrived
  in the market
mister
  your guile is wealth
  in winter
  your wealth is desolation
  in spring

All-American

She's an alabaster history
in complete shambles
        marble skulled
        blind eyed
        bright
her villains are lovers
at the ready
with detailed plots
and inexact maps
        I am her Lewis
        and Clark
            schizophrenic
and identifying with the Chinooks
on the Columbia
she's a beaver pelt mama
loving my All-American ambitions
on the way to the National Championship
        while sitting out
        the Sugar Bowl
in the voodoo shop watching
the black and white TV of forgotten
days
        we flicker the paradox of sharp focus
        past
with the end zone and Pacific in sight
I love her on the grand staircase
        of the museum
        made for Tzara's match
with tens of the thousands of Chinese
        tourists
up from their New Jersey hotels
        machine gunning
        cameras capturing
        every moment
        to delete
she is well tuned for a big break
        down

and once the drums start to pound
restless we'll make our way
to one of the better games
       in town

Jane in Her Business Suit

Jane in her business suit
jumping rope in the schoolyard
playing the game of allure
        and lost time
said that she'd pay extra
for the strongman to kick in
        her front door
wash her dirty sheets
and set six places at the table
for Wednesday afternoon's lunch

the circus so rarely came town
cotton candy was always in high demand
Jane's teeth were already beginning
        to rot but that was the way
of the neighborhood
she was quite willing to trade her suit
        for sweets
none of us were strongmen
but we had the cash necessary for candy .
though it set us back a week's wages

Jane without her business suit
let us swing her rope
while she worried about Wednesday's lunch
        and the places
that desperately needed to be set
her allure was of lost times
        both hers and ours
it was Tuesday morning
and we all knew that we'd be out of jobs
in the very near future

none of us were tired
so we didn't see the necessity
of busting down the front door
        to get to the dirty sheets
we all stripped sang

songs pulled out our loose
        and decaying teeth
collected slingshot stones
with sticky fingers and waited
for Wednesday's guests to arrive

This Being an Odd Day

This being an odd day:
        man slips
        on evolutionary
        banana peel,
        tumbles
        two flights,
        slapstick reignited.
This being an odd day:
        curators questioned
        in museum
        for lack of criteria
        and identification
        cards, no new
        doctorate
        theses to come.
This being an odd day:
        fifty degrees
        Fahrenheit dive,
        nation records
        record lows
        as government
        warns not to take
        plunge lightly
        and disregards
        global prerogative.

Market Day

Market day
            endives;
I laugh,
you smile,
            vegetarians
shop up the street
            sniffing clouds.
Your broken arm
            is beautiful.
Your black dress
            is not worth the trouble.
Your paring knife
            brings up memories
    of balance.
Your Sunday salad
            is Monday
    leftovers.

Cessation Special

The illuminated manuscripts
were transferred online for easy access
and all their pages pulped.
I left the book trade late
and went into the equally abysmal skin trade.
Scalded in the kitchen
I dined on fortune cookies
served up by harem girls, unionized.
Peg Legs decided to dance
and talked the whole time
of the golden age of DJs
back when West 8th Street was less noxious.
We both wept over Gray's Papaya
while reading the want ads,
eyes behind cheap sunglasses.

Outset and Onslaught

Magenta stockings morning
                         rise.
Your purple painted eyelids
           dawn the west
           so far east.
           The television
is turned off in the room fraught
           with the lost night policies
           of comfort. My eyes
are caught on the on switch,
the fan spins slowly
about to fall.

Luscious

Tapped onto   stage/d
      a burlesque odd
      she
      bowed
out before the applause
          ended
I see   no more need
     serve me Prosecco
     instead of Champagne
I tell you
I told them
      she is Lenten
      Ash Wednesday
      fish sandwiches
I don't care for salmon roe
her routine   lost in the wings
she   exact
      pigeon toed

Triangle

That was backstage
                Gdansk
                Greenpoint
                Milwaukee Avenue
dark eyelashes   fashionable chokers
    blue rooms
        and a reddening cold
    that thrilled all the dearly departing
    and cracked the made up masculinity
                in waning hours
        when the curtains rose
on the Pilsudski subterfuge
with Cinco de Mayo   Puebla furor
        back
    east
    the
    sun
    got
    to
    us
    first

She Was a Study in Wind Patterns

Studied
      her own(ed)
         (un)certainties
as/if/   scientifically
              method
      ortho/dox(ology)
as/it was
as/you were
as/I will be
      AAAAhhhh
She missed the men she knew
                 Street strut
            absolution(ist)
and I
      undermined
      determinate
docile and wind swept
      saturated
bomb/ast(ic)
      on corner
caught
            the addition
             (of)
two angles
                          ON THE far outside
                          sum(marized)
in stark light
           filled with shadows

Stoop Sale

Bought the subject
matter for success
at the stoop sale
and then fell back
in the garden
and grew fat
while she blasted
popular culture
on a summer afternoon
her springtime was
the stuff of photo albums
before tastes changed
she poured me
quinine lemonade
while smiling
at the sound
of mosquitoes buzzing
autumn would come
then winter snowstorms
Christmas presents
would remain unwrapped
and New Year's parties
would lose the thread
of their theme
she let her ball gown
drop and collected
on maladies
while I waited
fortunate

Lunch Break

Starched to stiff
the blue collar stained.
      Even lunch seems long today.
I wrote to the dead page
which is always pristine.
I requested that it bloody itself
      on the factory floor,
or at the least get a little frayed
      at the edges.
I am the sum total of my ham
and cheese sandwich. I am the sorry
      state
of affairs. I am another day
      digested
after hard, dry swallows.

El

Window   out   on elevated
       train tracked
the fast   laugh.
           Head hanging down,
but stomach   caught prosperity.

Your heart attack!

The children have got that blank stare
    that they get when
        they're talking
about where their parents will be tomorrow
    night.

I met know nothings   and they turned me over
to their bosses who were even more unaware
     as   they pulled the trap.

Down!

Thankfully I broke my back,
which merely resumed my boredom.

I don't search for egg sandwiches,
        or candy   bars   anymore
and I sleep easy
        knowing that   capitalism
is not compatible   with   Christianity

and laugh at penitents and pallbearers
who have their heads shaved at third rate barber shops
and brush their teeth on the way to fame
and forget to transfer at the right stop while they chatter
and cry at the approaching sight of the ocean.

Leopard Skin Coat

Blue & Gold Bar
     applause;
leopard
          skin
    coat,
I celebrate
    you
         before the crowd
    &   you
    delight.
Remember
    me
    in   your
    nightly
prayers.
        I
want the Africa
    of   you
    &   your
    kill,
    you
fashion famous
         with
fake eyelashes,
    you
         a mascara
    ad boy's
favorite reverie.
    Your
         marriage
shocks everyone
    who wants to be
shocked   and that's
    what
    you
told me to
    expect.

Frankie, the Airplanes Are Diving

Let —
      no
there was
            their
      Boris Karloff
look –
dashing
Frankenstein
              come down
JFK
      and caught the A
        all the way
           to Jay
Street to miss Manhattan's
        merry
        melodies
Borough Hall was (k)/no/w(n)
        more
MetroTech   morbid
             r   p
          e   a
        r   d
        cheat
        Chase
that was back when
Water Street wasn't worth it   know
          more
he was handsome
caught all the ladies who lunched
           in their
      night/gowns
        /mares
built skyscrapers out of their curves
    heinous
                hub
             bub
          of
        wanting

pretty girls
all fled Midtown desks
                        Frankie
                the airplanes are diving
down
elevator
escalator
bring —
        up   to speed

Still Dark

Last night late
at the dead end
you said
it was about dawn
too early to be stopped
in spite of the still dark
I didn't see
any clocks
but felt certain
in the one way back
it was a splendid
alley for movie posters
even if there
were no cinemas
in sight
such places are ideal
for daring
the perfect
environment
in which
to eat a peach
before heading
to the tailors
to be fitted
for deluge pants
here in
the United States
there are no
grand boulevards
worth the pomp
or walk
the side
streets set the tone
for the nation
between moon
and sun
and watch repair
shop shuttered

the end came
early in shadow
our static charged

Coney Island Solstice Extension

Let's ride bicycles
      on the highway on
      the Fourth of July
when everyone is worked
      up about fireworks
      and picnics
and the most patriotic way
      to fold the flag
      after mustard and ketchup
has dripped on it. Let's sing
      the Star-Spangled Banner
      on *le Quatorze Juillet*
and laugh about Louis XVI's bad investments.
      Let's throw the history books
      in the campfire for melting marshmallows
and forget about all the rewrites. Let's
      ignore the Assumption
      and enjoy the rest of August.
Let's trade the Pope's bad blood,
      the President's bleeding nose
      and all the prophets' chatter
for a ride on the Wonder Wheel.

www.ingramcontent.com/pod-product-compliance
Lightning Source LLC
Chambersburg PA
CBHW071804040426
42446CB00012B/2703